IF WE WERE HAVING COFFEE...

ISBN: 978-1-68088-183-7

▐ and Blue Mountain Press are registered in U.S. Patent and Trademark Office. Certain trademarks are used under license.

Printed in China.
First Printing: 2017

⊕ This book is printed on recycled paper.

This book is printed on paper that has been specially produced to be acid free (neutral pH) and contains no groundwood or unbleached pulp. It conforms with the requirements of the American National Standards Institute, Inc., so as to ensure that this book will last and be enjoyed by future generations.

Blue Mountain Arts, Inc.
P.O. Box 4549, Boulder, Colorado 80306

IF WE WERE HAVING COFFEE...

A Conversation About

FRIENDSHIP

written and illustrated by ronnie walter

Blue Mountain Press™
Boulder, Colorado

IF WE WERE HAVING COFFEE...

I'd tell you that you look gorgeous
in that particular shade of blue

or bright pink

or even that shade
of chocolate brown you
are so partial to...

because I want you to know

how beautiful
you are

...even on days that you don't think so.

(And, by the way, you do look awesome in blue.)

We might even talk about our hair
for a while and discuss if cutting
it off or growing it out
might be best.

We'd certainly talk about our diets
and why, with all our other
accomplishments, our weight seems
to be the one thing we can't
quite get a handle on.

Then we'd probably decide to
share a cranberry scone.

IF WE WERE HAVING COFFEE...

I'd tell you the most embarrassing thing that happened to me since we saw each other last, and we would both groan at the sheer humiliation of it all. That would remind us of more tales of embarrassment...

until we'd stop and realize how
darn human we are, not the
superwomen we envisioned we'd
be just a few years ago.

IF WE WERE HAVING COFFEE...

I'd listen to you tell me how
hard it was when you went
through those tough times,
and I would say,

"I know.

I know."

Then I would reach across the table
and touch your hand. Our eyes would
well up with tears, we'd look at
each other, and you would say,

"I know you know."

We would succeed at keeping it together as we took a sip of coffee and ate another bite of scone.

IF WE WERE HAVING COFFEE...

We'd go through the list of things that have irritated us lately...

like wet towels on the
bathroom floor and that
cranky woman at the bank
and, of course, the price
of gas and milk...

and why we never have time to just sit and read a book, for crying out loud. Then we'd take a drink of coffee and say,

"Boy, we've got it good,

don't we?"

IF WE WERE HAVING COFFEE...

You'd ask me how that thing I was working on was coming along. I'd say something like,

"You know I am so...
passionate
about that, but I'm not really
sure what to do about it."

And you'd tell me how talented
I am and how the world needs
my brilliance.

And maybe we'd spend
some time figuring out how
I can move forward and still
pay attention
to all my other
obligations.

Then I'd say,
"What about you?
How's that thing
you do going?"

You'd roll your
eyes and say,

"I don't know!
Am I wasting
my time?"

And my eyes would widen, and I'd put my coffee down and say,

"Are you nuts? That is exactly what you should be doing!

There! You have my permission!"

You would laugh and say,
"Why thank you!"

and then lift your cup
in a little salute.

We'd eventually start talking about other people and say things like,

"What was she thinking?"

and

"I feel so bad for them,"

and...

"When I get home,
I'll call her."

And we'd be quiet once
again for just a second, and
our hearts would hurt a little
because maybe we were being
a bit catty and not so kind...

or maybe we're just trying
to figure out why people
are the way they are,
and we'd think...

"I must be kinder.
I must be more
understanding."

We'd take a final sip of our coffee and scoop up the rest of the scone and then check our phones before we put them back in our bags.

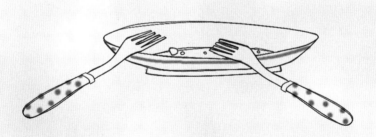

We'd say things like,

"This was really nice,"

and

"I needed this,"

and

"I miss you, you know?"

and

"Let's not wait so long next time."

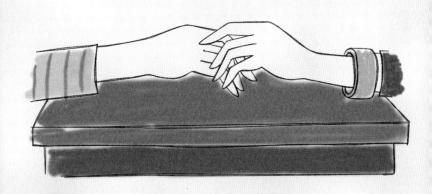

And we'd mean every
word of it.

We'd stand up, throw our
bags over our shoulders,
and hug each other.

Tightly.

IF WE WERE HAVING COFFEE.

ABOUT THE AUTHOR

From the first time she was handed a blank piece of paper and a crayon, Ronnie Walter knew what she wanted to do for a living—draw pictures and tell stories! She has been a successful artist and writer for over twenty years; her words and illustrations have been used for books, fabric, home accessories, gift items, greeting cards, and much more. Ronnie lives in a little house by the water with her husband and their rescue Catahoula Cur, Larry. She is frequently caffeinated.